A Writers Group Companion:

a twelvemonth of prompts and recipes

Deborah Auten

Up Yonder Books

2013

A Writers Group Companion: a twelvemonth of prompts and recipes
Deborah Auten

This book is published by Up Yonder Books
125 East Palace Avenue #72
Santa Fe, NM 87501
www.upyonderbooks.com
Copyright ©2013

ISBN-13: 978-0991216307
ISBN-10: 099121630X

Notice of Rights: All rights reserved. No part of this book may be reproduced or transmitted in any form by any mrans, electronic, mechanical, photocopying, recording, or otherwise, without the prior written permission of the publisher. For information on getting permission for reprints and excerpts, contact permissions@upyonderbooks.com.

Notice of Liability: The information in this book is distributed on an "As Is" basis, without warranty. While every precaution has been taken in the preparation of the book, neither the author nor Up Yonder Books shall have any liability to any person or entity with respect any loss or damage caused or alleged to be caused directly or indirectly by the instructions contained in this book.

Picture Credits/Notations:
All photographs and illustrations except for the recipe photographs are in the public domain with no known restrictions. All photographs other than the recipe photographs were recolored iand otherwise adapted in Photoshop by the author. All recipe photographs by the author.

Cover Photograph: "Oak Leaves" 1916 Yearbook, Vol. 13 MCMXVI, Meredith College, Raleigh, NC from J.C. Knowles Collection, State Archives of North Carolina.*
Back Cover Photograph: Am. Lib. Assoc. WWI book drive, New York Public Library; Theodore Wesley Koch papers, box 12, Folder: World War I, 1914-1918--ALA Activities*
January Thesaurus Day Photograph: Wikimedia Commons: 1930 International Pageant of Pulchritude, Photo originally by Joseph M. Maurer, Library of Congress Prints and Photo graphs Online. Picture originally was of Miss Universe (center), flanked by Miss Pittsburgh, Miss New York, Miss Detroit, Miss Russia, Miss Roumania, Miss New Jersey, and Miss Kentucky.
January Prompt Illustration: p. 33 The Domesday Book, from "Historic Byways and Highways of Old England", William Andrews, 1910.*
February Don't Cry Over Spilled Milk Day Photograph: "Portrait of a Young Woman," H. Allison & Co. Photographers, 1905.* No known restrictions as per the Public Record Office of Northern Ireland, the Allison Collection Images as posted on Flickr.
February Prompt Illustration: Illustration by Boris Artzybasheff from Verotchka's Tales by Dmitry Mamin-Sibiryak, published by E.P. Dutton, NY 1922.*
March Multiple Personality Day Photograph: Composite of the following photographs:
    Photo by Bains News Service from the Library of Congress Collection, the Bain Collection*
    "The Staging of La Boheme", 1865, The Staging of Artists in Photography of the 19th and 20th century, an exhibition, Museum Ludwig Koln*
    Emma Goldman, 1901 mugshot, from Wikimedia Commons, no known restrictions*
    The Double Exposure Collection, 1905, from thepublicdomainreview.org*
    "Wisham Girl, profile", 1910, Edward Curtis, Library of Congress*
March Prompt Illustration: Vintage Clip Art, circa 1880's, free download from the graphicsfairy.com*
April Fool's Day Photograph: "Arthur Price as Jester for the 'Pageant of Empire'", fP. B. Abey and Wallace Jones, Buith Wells Historical Pageant photo album, now in the public domain through the National LIbrary of Wales*
April Prompt Illustration: 1540, Heinrich Vogtherr the Younger, Narr mit Marotte, Kolorierter Holzschnitt von Heinrich Vogtherr dem Jüngeren, um 1540, Original uploader was Fotomusikus at de.wikipedia, (Original text : Gotha, Sammlungen des Schloßmuseums)*
May Mother Goose Day Photograph: "Ruth Draper", 1903,Library of Congress, Prints and Photographs Division, original photo by Francis Benjamin Johnston*
May Prompt Illustration: Denslow's Mother Goose, by W. W. Denslow, 1901, projectgutenberg.org*
June Celebration of the Senses Photograph: "Miss Marie Doro, No. 2", 1902, by Burr McIntosh, Library of Congress*
June Prompt Illustration: This clipart is derived from clip art that was released into the public domain by the Open Clip Art Library.
July Ugly Truck Day Photograph: no known copyright restrictions, Photographs of Old Lviv, Lvivskogo Beer, originally part of private collection*
July Prompt Illustration: from "The Gasoline Automobile" by George Hobbs, 1915.*
August National Thriftshop Day: Human Ecology Historical Photographs, 1921, Division of Rare and Manuscript Collections, Cornell University Library*
August Prompt Illustration: Victorian Tea Set, from thegraphicsfairy.com, from The Art Journal: The Industray of All Nations, Illustrated Catalogue, London England: Brad bury and Evans, 1851*
September Swap Ideas Day Photograph: "Telephone operator.png", Kibbe Hancock Heritage Museum, Carthage, Illinois, Flickr Collection
September Prompt Illustration: "The Creation of Adam," Sistine Chapel, Michaelangelo: photographs that reproduce a two dimensional public domain work are in the public domain (original photo modified from one downloaded through the Wikimedia Commons).
October Face Your Fears Day Photograph: Powerhouse Musuem Collection, 1895-1905, from the Flickr Free Collection.*
October Prompt Illustration: "Halloween Dance Clip Art", public domain image from Free Clip Art.
November Absurdity Day Photograph: Flickr Commons, photo contributed by jamasca66
November Prompt Illustration: From More Nonsense, Twenty-Six Nonsense Rhymes & Pictures, Edmund Lear, 1894, projectguntenberg.org*
December National Haiku Day Photograph: from Flickr Commons, uploaded by Alan Davey, photo by Elstner Hilton, circa 1914-1918*
December Illustration: Basho script, 17th C. poet

*Public Domain Notification: This work is in the public domain in the United STates because it was published (or registered with the U.S. Copyright Service) before January 1, 1923.

for Nadine, Catherine, Susan, Hope, Janie, Jillian & Barbara, and to Jennifer who began it all…

and for Sam and Hannah, for their patience and love

Introduction

My writers' group began as a seven week children's book writing and illustration workshop in January of 1999. We must be doing something right, because we're still here.

Originally, writer and illustrator Jennifer Owings Dewey was our teacher. We could turn in finished work each week to her for personal critique, but the structure of our weekly class was to have everyone write to a prompt Jennifer provided, which was usually based on a point of writing craft she wanted us to explore. Topics were diverse, and included themes like narrative description, showing not telling, the pitfalls of "had" and "but" and the use of any word ending in "ly." Eventually, there were more content-oriented prompts: writing a murder scene backwards, an obituary for our main character, and what would happen if someone wanted to join a circus to name a scant few.

When Jennifer moved away in November of 2009, we just kept going.

Our format is simple: someone brings a prompt each week, we write from forty-five minutes to an hour or more, and then depending on the number of people there, leaving the rest of the time for reading what we wrote and discussion.

Let me digress for a moment to emphasize something that might slip by in that prosaic description of what we do: writing together is the soul-time of the group. There is something alchemical about the profound silence during which we write as a group yet as individuals, each immersed in his or her own work. I'm aware some groups do this, and some don't. All I know is that to me, the act of writing side by side is power writing at its best, the tie that binds us.

The discussion that follows each person's reading is not only allowed but encouraged, perhaps a holdover of the original "class" idea. We have three precepts about these discussions. First, the comments should begin with a positive. Second, any criticism should be constructive. We depend on each other not only to maintain this standard of civility, but also to be honest if the writing induces confusion, needs an injection of emotion, or verges into "telling," purple prose, digression–you get the idea. Third, no one has to read aloud after writing time, or even work to the prompt if, for example, someone needs to work on a tricky scene or is putting finishing touches on an otherwise completed manuscript.

There's a fourth principle we try to live by as well, and I use the word "try" deliberately. We try not to interfere with the story itself too much. Sometimes we get excited and ideas come bubbling up–some of us enjoy that process while others don't. Most of us have been in the group long enough that we know who is tolerant of what. When someone new joins, we take time to make a safe place for that person to feel comfortable.

But how do recipes come into it, you ask? Almost as important as writing time are the first fifteen minutes (or so) to catch up on each other's lives. The person who provides the prompt also provides a "snack." While this can be cheese and crackers, fresh raspberries, or brownies, every once in a while someone cooks something special as a centerpiece. Food has therefore become a bond between us as well--we are not just a cut-and-dry, read-what-you-got and isn't-that-nice sort of group. We support each other through the thick and thin not only of the writing life, but of life itself, the everyday wear and tear on our souls. We've been through weddings and divorce, cancer and death, the birth of children and grandchildren, and survived the loss of still-sorely-missed members.

To do all this, we limit our group size to eight to ten and we ask for commitment to show up every week on Friday from four to six pm. No one is expected to be there every week and at times someone has taken a hiatus, but by and large we have five or six people almost all the time and often the full group is there.

There's a lot of other ways of having a writers' group out there: groups where you bring completed work, groups that don't allow comments, groups that forbid food and discourage chatter, groups that are come-when-you-want and may have as many as 25 or more members. What I've outlined above is what works for us–food most definitely included.

To that end, here is A Writers' Group Companion: a Twelvemonth of Prompts and Recipes, in the hopes that it will enliven one you already belong to or encourage you to start your very own.

Deborah Auten is a member of the Santa Fe Writers Group, which you can keep up with at www.santafewritersgroup.com and on Facebook, the Santa Fe Writers Group. She is currently working on a literary fiction novel and a nice, fluffy "cozy" mystery.

Thesaurus Day : January 18th

This is the birthday of Peter Roget, born in 1779, King of Synonyms (adequation, agreement, alikeness, compatibility, conformity, correlation, correspondence, equality, evenness, exchangeability, identity, interchangeability, interchangeableness, likeness, match, par, parallel, parity, synonymy).

Finding that exact (right, perfect, precise...) word for me is one of the joys of writing—so much so that my preferred word processing program is WordPerfect 8, with the best built-in thesaurus I've ever found in a word processing program, bar none. I coddle my old disk like it's a Ukrainian Easter Egg.

The thesaurus can also be overused (go to extremes; carry too far...you get the idea).

But what about the deeper meaning of the idea of thesaurus? The themes of the word synonym include the idea of substitution, of things that are almost the same but not quite, and also the idea of suggestion.

Prompts:

1) Write about a situation where someone tries to substitute one thing for another, but is found out.

2) Create a dialogue in which one person takes the words of the other and subtly twists them to change the other person's point of view to their own.

3) The thesaurus is one of those can't-live-without writer's tools that can also be part of the old standby when you are really stuck: close your eyes, open a page and pick a word at random, using it to get you going.

Banana Almond Muffins (with substitutions)

Ingredients

2 cups unbleached flour (you may substitute sorghum flour or oat flour)
½ cup sugar (or the equivalent in honey)
½ cup oatmeal (umm…maybe buckwheat?)
2 tsp. baking powder (or 1 1/3 tsp. cream of tartar and 2/3 tsp baking soda)
1 tsp. baking soda (or 2 more tsp. of baking powder)
1 tsp. of nutmeg (or 1 tsp. of pumpkin pie spice)
1 tsp. of vanilla (or 1 tsp. of almond extract)
½ cup unsweetened applesauce (or ½ cup of pureed apples or peaches)
1 egg (or 1/4 cup of egg substitute)
½ cup buttermilk (or ½ cup of milk and 1 tbsp of either yogurt or lemon juice - let stand for a few minutes)
½ ripe bananas (or the equivalent in very, very ripe peaches)

Preparation

Preheat oven to 375 degrees. Grease a muffin tin.

Mix dry ingredients together in one bowl, wet ones in another.

Add wet to dry and mix until all ingredients are just combined.

Fill each muffin tin to about two-thirds full. Bake for 15 minutes, then test for doneness with a tooth pick or knife. Bake longer if necessary. Remove from tin and cool.

Don't Cry Over Spilled Milk Day: February 11th

No regrets. Move on. Get over yourself. The past is the past.

Regret is motivation. Regret can lead to despair and death, especially if you are John Updike, or like characters whose past errors or losses eat them from the inside out. There's certainly a whole genre of modern literature that thrives on the idea of soul-twisting endings and unresolved, and therefore never-ending conflict.

But must regret always be futile? The power of regret can also be harnessed to bring a character redemption and salvation. Isn't this the story arc we all want in our real lives—even if you are someone who doesn't require it in your books?

Prompt Ideas:

1) Wallow in regret: that is to say, load a character up with all the regrets you can think of, and put that character in a scene with someone else. Does the character turn into a caricature? Or, is the regretful character brave and determined though regretful? How does the regret show itself? How does it affect the other person?

2) "I could have done more..." is a quintessential phrase of regret. Create a scene around this idea. If it's flashback, work to make the sense of regret immediate and relevant to the current tension or conflict, weaving the story into a dialogue rather than having the flashback be "told."

3) Create a failure in a character's backstory. Use it to show how it changed the character, via action rather than narrative.

Tres Leches Cake (Three Milk) with Pinon Nuts

Cake:
1 ½ teaspoons baking powder
1/4 teaspoon salt
1 cup all-purpose flour
5 large eggs, separated, room temperature
1 cup sugar
1/3 cup milk
1 teaspoon almond extract
1 cup pinon nuts

Tres Leches Mixture:
1/4 cup heavy cream
One 14-ounce can sweetened condensed milk
One 12-ounce can evaporated milk

Topping (optional):
1 cup pinon nuts
1/4 c. sugar
1 tbsp. butter
½ tsp. almond extract

Directions

Preheat the oven to 350 degrees. Butter well a 9- by 13-inch cake pan, then dust with flour.

Put flour, baking powder and salt into a sifter and sift into a large bowl. Separate the eggs. Beat the yolks on high speed with hand mixer. Add 3/4 cup of the sugar gradually. Beat until the yolks turn pale yellow. Stir in the milk and vanilla. Pour this mixture over the flour mixture and stir gently to combine all elements.

Toast the pinon nuts in a dry skillet until golden, then stir into batter. In a separate bowl, beat the egg whites (high speed with hand mixer or by hand) until they form soft peaks. Gradually add the remaining 1/4 cup sugar. This time, beat on high speed until egg whites are stiff, but don't overbeat them into a dry state. Fold the egg white mixture into the batter, very delicately. Pour carefully into the prepared sheet pan, and spread with spatula until even.

Bake 35 to 40 minutes. Test with a knife or toothpick for doneness. Allow to cool. Turn pan upside down onto a platter with an edge to contain the tres leches mixture.

To make the tres leches: Combine the cream and the two milks in a small pitcher. With a skewer or fork, pierce the cake all over. Pour the tres leches mixture evenly over the cake. Allow the cake to sit for at least several hours in the refrigerator until ready to serve.

To make the topping, combine sugar butter and almonds. Stir until golden brown and add nuts. Pour onto greased pan and allow to cool. Crumble over cake.

Multiple Personality Day: March 5th

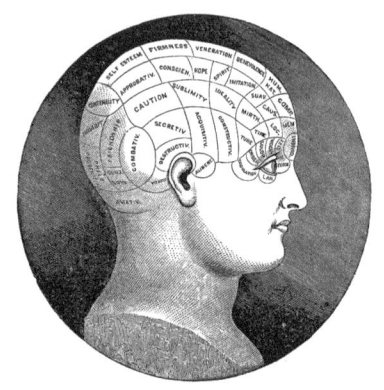

"Multiple Personality Day is an opportunity to get in touch with yourselves."
    –from holidayinsights.com

Multiple Personality, now known as Dissociate Identity Disorder, has caused a split in the therapy community: Some therapists believe in it, others don't.

But who would argue that we each have different sides to ourselves, that sometimes we behave impulsively in ways that surprise even ourselves? There's something called the Johari Window.

The Johari Window is a diagram created by Joseph Luft and Harrington Ingham in 1955 to understand both how we see ourselves and how others see us. Here it is in simple form:

What we know about ourselves *and* others also know about us	What we know about ourselves that others do *not* know about us
What others know about us that we don't see in ourselves	The unknown: What *neither* we nor others know about ourselves

So, in a sense, at least if you believe in the ideas the Johari Window lays out, we all have a version of multiple personalities.

PROMPTS:

1) Have a character completely flip personality in a scene: make a villain vulnerable, make a bully scared, turn a sweet person into a sour one...you get the idea. Even if only for a short scene, even if only as an exercise, this can suggest more depth to your character, more layers.

2) Create a scene in which someone overhears other people talking about him or her without being aware the person is listening. What will the eavesdropper find out about how they think of him/her and how does that affect the character?

3) What secret is a character hiding about him or herself?

Multiple Personality Bacon Bread

This bread can be either savory or sweet. What better choice for a great BLT? As toast, it's great with apricot jam or alternatively, try it with cream cheese and tomato with a little balsamic drizzled over. It makes a superb Pain Perdu, the fancy name for French toast: let it dry out a little, slice it thick, let it soak in an egg-cream mix 4-5 minutes on each side, fry and serve with maple syrup.

Ingredients: Makes one loaf

1 envelope yeast
1+ tbsp. sugar (can use brown sugar for a sweeter bread)
1 1/4 c. warm water
scant 1 tsp. salt
3 1/4 +/- cups of flour
1/4 cup of bacon drippings + enough to oil dough later
1 pound of bacon, sliced in narrow strips, cooked

Preparation

Mix gently envelope of yeast plus sugar in ½ cup of the warm water. Wait until it bubbles.

Once the yeast bubbles, add the rest of the warm water to it. Then add in the salt-flour mixture and blend well. Put this in a covered bowl in a warm place and let it rise for 30 minutes.

After it's risen, mix in the rest of the flour and salt (mix these together first), bacon grease and bacon. You might be able to use a mixer for this part, but if it's too stiff, beat with a fork. Once this is incorparated, add the rest of the flour, just enough so that the dough forms a ball and doesn't stick to the sides of the bowl. Then flour a board and knead for 5 minutes, until the imprint of a thumb bounces back reasonably well. If the dough gets sticky during kneading, add more flour to the board, which will be incorporated as you knead. Oil the dough with either regular oil (canola or vegetable) or with additional bacon grease. Put the dough in an oiled bowl, cover it and let it rise for an hour.

Once risen again, take the dough out and form it into a loaf and put it in a greased loaf pan. Let this rise again for 30 minutes.

The Fool's Day : April 1

April Fool's Day may be the echo of great unbridled dances below full moons when the drear of just staying alive was only bearable when you knew there was one day given over to going wild. In our time, it's meant to be a day of pranks, which range from switching the sugar and the salt to the 1957 epic BBC prank broadcast about the Swiss Spaghetti Harvest.

Let's not forget the Fool in April Fool's Day. Fools occupy a hallowed place in literature. Isaac Asimov put it perfectly in his Guide to Shakespeare: '...the great secret of the successful fool – that he is no fool at all.' Fools are foils, acting as both keen observer and sharp wit.

Prompt Ideas:

1) Write about a prank gone horribly wrong.

2) Fools are always secondary characters. What if the Fool was a main character? What depth can you bring to the Fool?

3) Let a character that is otherwise prim, repressed or depressed to...go wild.

Fruity Fool

What better dish for April Fool's than the traditional British dessert Fool? Fool can be made with virtually any kind of fruit (as long as it's mashed and seeded). Frozen fruit works quite well for this dish. Originally, the fruit was—gooseberries, naturally.

Ingredients: About 4-6 servings, depending on the appetite

1 cup of fruit, (suggestions: raspberries, strawberries, blackberries mangoes, kiwi)
1 tbs. sugar (approximately)
1 ½ tsp. lemon or lime juice
1 cup of heavy cream, chilled
½ tsp. vanilla (if you are feeling adventurous, try almond flavor instead)
Additional sugar to taste

Preparation

Mash/puree fruit. Push through strainer, if needed, to remove any seeds. If using fresh fruit, put in a bowl with sugar and lemon or lime juice.

Whip into soft peaks.

Fold in vanilla and fruit, GENTLY. Taste. Some fruits will have enough natural sugar, others won't. The only way to get the right balance of sugar is to taste.

Serve in a clear bowl if you have one.

Bonus: Sprinkle some toasted nuts over top for crunch and/or a hint salt. Suggestions: pine nuts, almonds or candied pecans.

Mother Goose Day : May 1

Whether you think Mother Goose is an archetype going back to cave paintings or the French spinner-of-tales "La Mére Oye", there's no doubt these are some of the first stories a child hears. Mother Goose rhymes, like fairy tales, embed themselves in our minds. Like fairy tales, some of them are frightening when you go past the pretty singsong of the verse and read what they say: think of Rock-a-Bye Baby, Ladybug and Humpty-Dumpty, to name just a few of the well-known ones.

Prompt Ideas:

1) Pick a favorite and use it as a jumping off point for a scene: What if London Bridge really did fall down?

2) I've always found this to be one of the most poignant of nursery rhymes:

Monday's child is fair of face,
Tuesday's child is full of grace;
Wednesday's child is full of woe,
Thursday's child has far to go;
Friday's child is loving and giving,
Saturday's child works hard for its living;
But the child that is born on the Sabbath day
Is bonny and blithe, and good and gay.

What happens when Wednesday's child meets Friday's? Just how far and through what does Thursday's child have to go?

3) Write a scene in which a blithe surface masks a dark reality.

Rustic Egg Tart

Mother Goose on Eggs:
In marble walls as white as milk,
Lined with a skin as soft as silk,
Within a fountain crystal clear,
A golden apple doth appear;
No doors there are to this stronghold,
Yet thieves break in and steal the gold.

Ingredients

For the pastry:
2 cups of flour
1 ½ tsp. salt
1 cup of chilled butter, cut in pieces
Chill water, approx. 1/4 c.
1 tsp vinegar

For the custard:
4 eggs
1 1/3 cup yogurt
½ tsp. salt

Filling #1:
3/4 cup shredded of Gruyere, Emmenthaler or Swiss cheese
6-8 slices ripe tomato

Filling #2:
3/4 cup shredded of Gruyere, Emmenthaler or Swiss cheese
cooked spinach, all water squeezed out

Mix flour and salt together. Separate slices of butter and put in flour. Use a food processor or your hands to mix the butter into the flour, so that you have peas-size granules in the bowl. Add the vinegar to the water and mix until the dough holds together. Chill in the refrigerator about 30 minutes.

Preheat oven to 380 degrees. The pastry above should be enough for two small or one large tart. When dough is chilled, divide in two sections and roll out on floured board in a rough circle. Lay round in pie plate - do not trim edges.

For spinach tart, place spinach in bottom of pie, then layer with cheese. For cheese and tomato tart, start with the cheese and reserve tomato until you add the custard. Add enough custard to each tart to cover ingredients. (For the cheese and tomato tart, then layer tomatoes in circular pattern on top.) Then fold the irregular edges of the pie dough over the custard. Pleat the dough as necessary as you fold it over the filling.

Bake tarts for 35 minutes and then check to see if dough and top are browning. If necessary, leave in for additional 5 minutes increments, checking each time.

Celebration of the Senses Day: June 24th

Writing with loving attention to the senses can bring life and depth to any descriptive narrative. If a scene feels flat, linger over a taste, smell or touch that might not only give an added dimension to the scene, but to the characters involved through their reactions to that taste, smell or touch, whether it's pleasant or horrid. Remember that the absence of a sense may be equally important.

Remember also that sometimes the celebration of the senses is for you as a writer - this might equally be a "prompt" for you if you are blocked, casting around for ideas lost in the depths of your subconscious. If that's the case, get out of your usual chair and go treat yourself to a sense: page through a photography book or website online, crush some fresh basil or rosemary under your nose, close your eyes and listen to your favorite music, or take a moment to rub that wonderfully smelly lotion you keep on your desk onto your neck and face so you can keep smelling it for hours—when you get back to work, refreshed. Lavish some time on the process, reveling as much as possible in your senses.

Prompts

1) One of my first breakthroughs as a writer was when Jennifer Owings Dewey set our class to the following exercise: Find a photograph and begin by describing minutely every aspect of the subject trying to cover each and every one of the senses. Do not try to make a story, the idea is to make the photograph real for someone who can't even see it. Using what you wrote first, now create a story.

2) Create a walk-on character for your story whose main characteristic is one that engages one or more senses of your protagonist. Dwell on their effect with creative detail.

3) Create a walk on character for your story whose main characteristic is the loss of a sense: they are deaf, blind, have anosmia (inability to smell), ageusia (inability to taste) or even congenital analgesic (inability to feel pain). How does this change or inform the scene, the other characters, or even the story itself?

Bonus: Blindfold yourself and try to navigate your own home. Try to make yourself a simple meal or pick out an outfit and put it on.

Salty Sweet Chile Toffee

This recipe is simple, but appeals to all the senses: the toffee with the chunks of nuts is highlighted with red, the surface of the toffee is buttery and smooth, the smell will be heady, it should break with a satisfying crack, and best of all, you'll have hot, sweet, and salty on your tongue.

Ingredients

2 cups butter
1 2/3 cups sugar
1/4 c. light corn syrup
1/4 teaspoon chunky salt
Red chile pepper to taste
Chunky salt to taste (such as a fleur de sel or other specialty salt)
½ cup nuts: suggestions are cashews, almonds, peanuts or pinon nuts

Preparation

In a large heavy bottomed pan (a wide almost skillet-like pan might work well for this recipe), combine the butter, sugar, syrup and salt. Cook over medium heat, stirring until the butter is melted. Allow to come to a boil, and cook until the mixture becomes a dark amber color, and the temperature has reached 285 degrees F (137 degrees C). Stir often but not constantly, but be careful not to allow the mixture to separate. If it does, try a different stroke with your spoon and have some water ready to add in small amounts to try to bring the mixture back together.

If you don't have a thermometer, there's an old fashioned method: drop small amounts of the mixture into cold water - if it separates into small brittle threads, it's ready.

While the toffee is cooking, slather butter on a cookie sheet (the alternative would be a baking mat).

When ready, stir in the nuts, then pour the toffee onto the prepared baking sheet. Immediately sprinkle the chunky salt onto the surface, followed by the red chile pepper. Put the toffee in the refrigerator to chill until set. You can break it into pieces, but you can also let everyone break off their own. IF there's any left, store in an airtight container.

J·U·L·Y
Ugly Truck Day

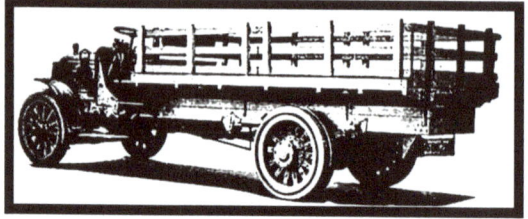

Ugly Truck Day : July 20th

Ugly trucks do the heavy lifting in life. Another dent in the side? Left out in the pouring rain? Just through in another load of horse manure and cement blocks.

Some ugly trucks are ugly because they've had a long, hard life. Some come off the drawing board that way, the kind of design that makes you wrinkle up your nose even if the paint is shiny and new.

Yet ugly trucks have their day. There's a lot of Ugly Truck Contests out there, and the best of them often are "Frankenstein" trucks, where the multicolored doors, bumpers and hoods that speak of raids on junk yards means that not just one but four or five ugly trucks live on.

I myself have a sneaking fondness for ugly trucks. A picture of one inspired the beginning of the book closest to my soul.

Prompts

1) Introduce an ugly truck, with or without an owner, into a scene and see what it does for the humor or pathos of the story. (What if a pretty girl owns it? What if a 92 year old granny owns it?)

2) I'd seen that truck before, somewhere on a back road when lightning crackled running over the frogs that littered the road in the pouring rain or maybe it lurking in the back of a nightmare, where I was one of the frogs...(Take it from here...)

3) If you had a character who was an ugly truck, who would that character be? What would they look like? What would their story be?

Pigs in a Blanket (Improved Version)

Trucks (no matter how they look) and tailgating go hand in hand. The right finger-food? Pigs in a Blanket!

Ingredients

1 package crescent roll dough
Proscuitto
Gruyure (or Swiss Cheese)

Preparation

Unroll triangles of dough. Cut each triangle in half. Cut cheese into 1/4" x 1/4" x 2" slices, enough for each triangle you have. Wrap ½ slice of prosciuto (or pancetta) around the cheese. Place wrapped prosciuto and cheese along long side of one triangle. Roll up so that end of the roll is the tip of the triangle.

Bake at 350 degrees for 12-15 minutes.

Eat.

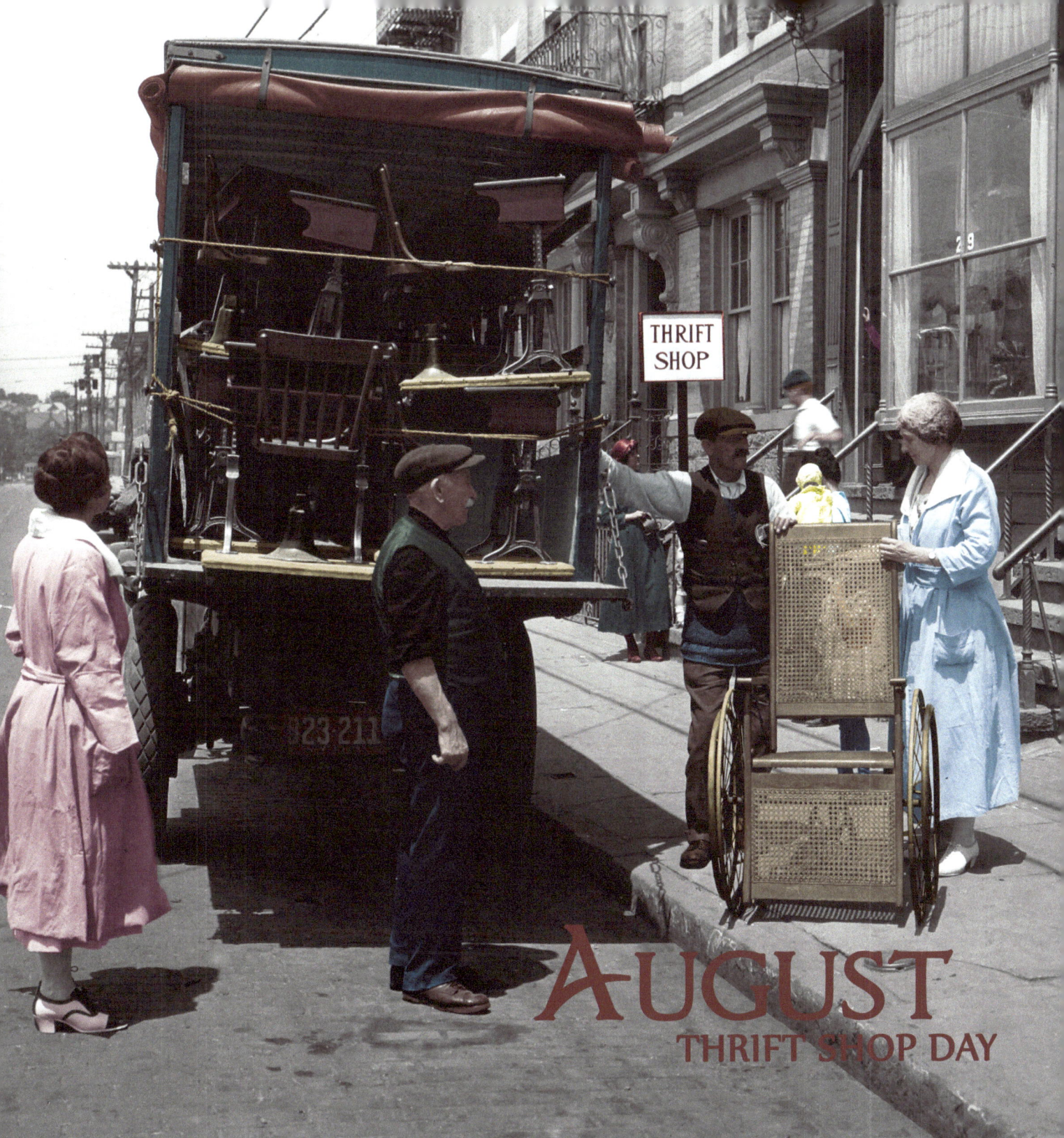

August
THRIFT SHOP DAY

National Thriftshop Day : August 17th

You never know what you will find. In May of 2012, a woman bought a painting for $10 at the Goodwill. It turned out to be from a Russian abstract painter, and was valued at $20,000. On the other hand, you can end up buying an old plate for $1.00 that's worth 50 . I have an old lamp I've carted around since college that I imagine has no value at all except to me. All my thrift shop finds fall into this category. These days I have to look hard—it's more of a treasure hunt than ever because there's a lot of drek—but that makes the finding more satisfying.

Prompts

1) Get out of your chair (that's right, you can do it). Go to a thrift store (either your favorite or one you have never been to before). Poke, peer, prod. Find something (don't forget the old book section). Maybe it's a single etched glass punch cup (did someone smash all the others when they were left at the altar? Is it the last vestige of wealth from an aging matriarch?) Maybe it's a piece of crazy costume jewelry, an old eight track tape, or a yellowing wedding dress. Let your found object be an inspiration for a new story or a new twist on an existing one.

2) Thrift stores sometimes have old postcards and notecards. Have one character write a note to another—perhaps writing something that would be better said face to face.

3) What if one character gave away another's possessions to a thrift store?

Bruschetta Seconda

Bruschetta is basically slices of bread that is rubbed with garlic then topped with something chopped, which usually includes tomatoes. Seconda means seconds, which in this case means to take all those halves of vegetables, single carrots, that lone leftover corn on the cob and almost-too-ripe-for-anything else tomatoes and make what we shall call, for dressing-up's sake, a vegetable tapenade.

Ingredients

A loaf of French Bread (buy day old if you want to continue in the thrift vein)

Possible vegetable ingredients: olives, corn, carrots, onion, capers, cucumber, red/green/yellow peppers, red pepper can be chopped finely fresh; zucchini, eggplant and mushrooms should be sliced and sautéed first.

A few cloves of garlic

Olive oil

Balsamic Vinegar

Preparation

Chop ingredients finely, but don't pureé, which can turn everything into grey mush. A hand chopper is helpful here (which you may be lucky enough to find in a thrift store). Add vinegar and oil to taste (go gently and gradually adding the vinegar).

Slice bread in thick slices. Lightly toast or grill slices of bread.

Rub cut cloves of garlic on surface of bread slices. Put a dollop of vegetable tapenade on each.

Place on vintage-find plate from thrift store and serve.

Swap Ideas Day : September 10th

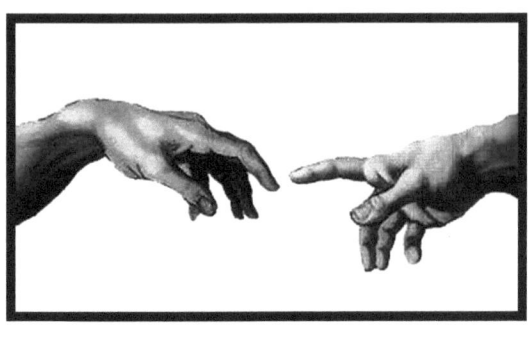

Writing groups are not just a sounding board, but also is a place for the constructive swapping of ideas—where to submit a manuscript, the name of a good copy-editor, or how to plug that hole in your mystery plot. There's also something to the idea of swapping life stories, whether with people you know or with complete strangers you will never see again, prying open the lid to your view of the world just a little wider.

Prompts

1) Have someone in your story be stuck for a long time, in a car or other limited space, with someone they know and don't like. Let the unliked person tell a story.

2) Have everyone in your writer's group (or four or five people you know) to write down a scene idea on a scrap of paper. Mix them up and draw one to use as inspiration.

3) If you are really brave, go to a laundromat, get on a bus, or go to a meetup (see www.meetup.com and search for a group in your area). Talk to someone you don't know and see if you can get them talking (So what was your favorite thing to do as a child? How about these young people today? If you could go back and relive your life, what would you do differently?) Take note of who they are, look beyond your own prejudices, make a mind-painting of every detail. As soon as you can, write down their description and something interesting they said to use in a story.

Trio of Swapped Dips

Swap Out:
Artichoke Dip
for Spinach and Sour Cream

Preheat oven to 375 degrees.

You may use marinated artichoke hearts for a more tart flavor, unmarinated for more subtlety.

12 oz. artichoke hearts
1/2 cup mayonnaise
2/3 cup parmesan or reggiano cheese, grated
Salt to taste
(Optional small amount of sour cream)

Put elements in blender and process. (I like to blend enough to mix the ingredients but so that the artichokes looked chopped instead of minced or pureed.) Put in ovenproof casserole dishes (ramekins will work). Bake for 25 minutes or until bubbly (less time if multiple, small ramekins are used).

Serve with crackers or French bread

Swap Out:
Black Bean Dip
for Hummus

1 can of black beans (or an equivalent amount of cooked black beans)
1 tsp. cumin
2 tbsp. olive oil
Salt to taste
1 tsp. lime juice

Put elements in food processor and puree until all ingredients are smooth. Turn out into serving bowl (no cooking required). Top with chopped tomatoes or red peppers - something red for contrast.

Serve with tortilla chips or flatbread.

Swap Out:
Cucumber Yogurt Dip with Cilantro Pesto
for Sour Cream and Onion

For the Cucumber Yogurt Dip
1 cup Greek Yogurt
½ c. chopped cucumber
1 tbsp. chopped dill
1 ½ tsp. lemon juice

Combine in a bowl and refrigerate.

For the Cilantro Pesto (this is supposed to work even for people who have the gene that turns the taste of cilantro into soap):

1 c. of chopped cilantro
1 large clove of garlic
1/4 cup of toasted almonds
1/4 cup of extra virgin olive oil
1/4 cup of hard cheese like Romano

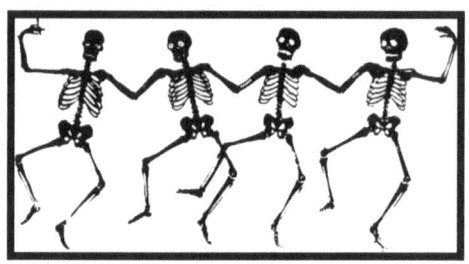

Face Your Fears Day: Third Tuesday in October

We owe this holiday to Steve Hughes, who teaches people to speak (speaking in public is often #1 in surveys). We write for the public, and sometimes I wonder just how different that is—unlike public speaking we (generally) don't face an audience, but most audiences will applaud politely, at the least. Writers, however, have to face critics, and those opinions can follow your book around.

Facing your fears, literally or in your literature, is a powerful tool.

Prompts

1) Take this one personally. Are you afraid of the blank page? The muddy middle? The unresolved end of your story? Tackle it now. NOW.

2) What is your main character's greatest fear? An axiom of writing is to create tension on every page. If you're writing suspense, you can use action. If you aren't, this gets harder. If your character has a phobia, particularly about something ridiculous, like phobophobia, which is the fear of developing a phobia, you can use that to explore the darker side of your character as well as to create tension when there's too much of a lull.

3) What if your character had a long-buried fear from some childhood terror that resurfaces?

Croissants

The Joy of Cooking says it best: "Rich, somewhat troublesome but unequaled by any other form of roll."

The "somewhat troublesome" croissant routinely shows up on lists of most difficult to bake, most fearful to make, and the like. In part this is because of the many steps involved, in part because this is because there is a certain amount of finesse involved. Then there is the matter of time–you may only work a portion of the actual time it takes to make these (time estimates range from 12 to 14 hours), but croissants also require that frenemy of writers, time.

Ingredients
 2 tablespoons all-purpose flour
 1 1/2 cups unsalted butter, at room temperature

 4 cups all-purpose flour, divided
 1/2 teaspoon salt
 3 tablespoons sugar
 2 (.25 ounce) packages active dry yeast
 1/4 cup lukewarm water
 1 cup milk
 1/2 cup heavy cream

 1 egg
 1 tablespoon water

Directions
Cut butter in slices and put in bowl. Sprinkle 2 tbsp. flour over, and combine with your hands. Put butter on a length of parchment paper, cling wrap or wax paper and form into 6 inch square. Fold into a packet and refrigerate 2 hours.

Dissolve the yeast in the 1/4 cup of lukewarm water. Set aside until it froths, between five and ten minutes. Mix 2 cups of the flour with the salt and sugar in a mixing bowl. Then, combine the milk and heavy cream into a small saucepan and warm ONLY to lukewarm (no more than 100 degrees). Once the yeast is frothy, add yeast and milk-cream mixture to the flour and stir.
Stir in the remaining 2 cups of flour 1/4 cup at a time to form a soft dough. Once dough is no longer sticky, knead the dough on a lightly floured work surface. Knead until smooth, about 5 minutes. Put dough back in bowl and cover with cling wrap. Refrigerate for 1 hour.

Next is the rolling and folding process, critical to the success of the croissants. Both the butter and the dough must be chilled. Roll the dough on a floured surface into a 10-inch square. Set the block of butter diagonally on the dough. Fold each corner of dough to the center of the square of butter, overlapping edges. Pinch edges together.

Starting from the center, working outward, roll the dough into a rectangle. This starts the laminating process of multiplying layers of butter and dough. The butter should be just at the temperature to roll into the dough. Wrap the dough in plastic and refrigerate again, until dough is chilled. Roll into a long 8 x 18 rectangle. Fold the dough into thirds, like a letter.

If the dough is still cool, you can make another fold. If not, again wrap and refrigerate, again folding like a letter. Then wrap and refrigerate for a minimum of 45 minutes. Let it warm slightly before rolling it out again. Remove the dough from the refrigerator and let it warm up for about 10 minutes before you begin rolling it out again. This time, make a long rectangle, then fold both ends to meet in the middle. Fold again in the middle. The dough will be very thick. Wrap and refrigerate for 1 to 2 hours. When you remove the dough, let it rest 20 minutes and again fold into thirds. This time refrigerate for at least 4-6 hours or overnight. plastic and refrigerate for 4-6 hours or overnight.

Roll the dough into a 10- by 38-inch rectangle on a lightly floured work surface, but do not roll it less than 1/4 inch thick. Use a sharp paring knife to trim rough edges of the dough. Divide the rectangle in half so that you have about two 5-inch wide strips of dough. Mark each strip into triangles, about 5 inches wide at the base. Cut the triangles and put onto parchment-lined baking sheets. Chill for 15 to 20 minutes.

Starting at the base of the triangle, roll the dough up gently. Be sure to put the tip of the triangle under the croissant so it doesn't unroll in the oven. Bend corners to make a crescent shape. Arrange on sheet and allow to rise until doubled, about 1 to 2 hours.

Preheat an oven to 425 degrees F. Beat the egg and small amount of water to make an egg wash. Brush the croissants and bake in oven until deep brown, approximately 22 to 25 minutes. You may need to extend baking time if center of croissants are unbaked. Cool on a rack before serving.

Absurdity Day : November 20th

There is a theory which states that if ever anybody discovers exactly what the Universe is for and why it is here, it will instantly disappear and be replaced by something even more bizarre and inexplicable. There is another theory which states that this has already happened.
—Douglas Adams, Hitchhiker's Guide to the Galaxy

Did you know there is philosophical theory called Absurdism, which is about how humans (try to) seek the meaning of life despite their total inability to do so? Douglas Adams is far more understandable than Kierkegaard or Camus, but writers have been struggling with this idea for a long, long time.

Then again, maybe that's just silly or incredibly unreasonable—absurd, as a matter of fact.

Prompts

1) One of my favorite personal examples of the absurd is the daughter of my first babysitter. Every day she would show up in some outrageous costume, a tiara and a paint-stained shirt over a tutu and flannel pajama bottoms, carrying a spatula, for example. Somehow she seemed attuned to some mystery of life, which reminded me to find some of that myself. Can you imbue a character with a dose of absurdity? Even a walk-on character can be a welcome break from a sad story, or a poignant one in a comedy.

2) Have someone do something completely out of character—an absurd act, at least for that person.

3) Create an absurd landscape for a scene.

Bonus: Go to www.bulwer-lytton.com. Edward George Bulwer-Lytton, wrote the famous first line: "It was a dark and stormy night..." but do you know how the rest of it goes? Over at the above website, they have a contest that is always open, to submit a single sentence in the "spirit" of the above to begin a fictional book. If you need to laugh, read the winners. The challenge: enter yourself.

Parmesan over Dark Chocolate

The Huffington Post reported that it has been "scientifically proven" that parmesan cheese and dark chocolate are a perfect pair. (Remember that people once thought prosciutto and melon were odd.) People are going crazy with recipes for chocolate tagliatelle with parmesan cream, and grilled parmesan and dark chocolate sandwiches.

We are going to keep the absurdity simple.

Ingredients

Your favorite dark chocolate
Your favorite parmesan cheese

Preparation

Break chocolate into two or four piece hunks. Take your grater or cheese slicer, and make thin slices of the parmesan. Stack. Serve.

Bonus: Check out www.foodpairing.com if you want to get much, much fancier—and even more absurd.

Bonus Bonus: Look up the recipe for potato chips dipped in chocolate and sea salt and drizzled in caramel.

National Haiku Day : December 21st

Haiku has three lines, the first and last with only five on (phonetic sounds, the idea of which in English we generally represent as syllables) the middle with seven: one of the most spare of all literary forms. The idea of haiku began with the word "cutting" in Japanese, kiru. In those three lines, the idea to show a juxtaposition of ideas:

Shizukasa ya   Calm and serene
Iwa ni shimi-iru   The sound of a cicada
Semi no koe   Penetrates the rock
                                    --Basho

While nature and the seasons are usually part of traditional haiku, haiku has predictably evolved to embrace today's nature:

The Web site you seek
Cannot be located, but
Countless more exist.

Not exatly about nature, but juxtaposition of ideas is still there.

Prompts

1) Begin a scene that takes the reader to a place of quiet. Create an action that flips the scene to an opposite.

2) Place your character in a natural scene where they learn a great lesson.

3) Take your character to a haiku reading.

Green Tea Cookies with Sesame Seeds

Ingredients

2 cups (10 ounces) all-purpose flour
½ teaspoon baking powder
½ teaspoon salt
3 tbsp. Macha (green tea powder)
16 tablespoons (2 sticks) unsalted butter, softened but still cool
1 cup (8 ounces) granulated sugar, plus 1/4 cup for rolling dough
1 large egg
1½ teaspoons vanilla extract
1/4 c. toasted sesame seeds

Preparation

Heat the oven to 375 degrees F. Line 2 large baking sheets with parchment paper or spray them with non-stick cooking spray.

Whisk the flour, baking powder, salt and Macha together in a medium bowl; set aside.

Cream the butter and sugar together at medium speed with a hand mixer until light and fluffy, about 3 minutes, using a rubber spatula to scrape the sides of the bowl. Add the egg and vanilla, also beating at medium speed briefly. Add the dry ingredients and beat at low speed until combined.

Place the 1/4 cup sugar and the sesame seeds for rolling in two shallow bowls. Fill a medium bowl halfway with cold tap water. Dip your hands in the water and shake off any excess (this will prevent the dough from sticking to your hands and ensure that the sugar sticks to the dough). Roll a heaping tablespoon of dough into a 1½-inch ball between moistened palms, dip the ball in the sugar first, then in the sesame seeds and place it on the prepared baking sheet. Repeat, spacing the balls about 2 inches apart. Flatten the dough balls with the buttered bottom of a glass until they are about ¾ inch thick.

Bake until the center of the cookies are just set, about 15 to 18 minutes, rotating the baking sheets front to back and top to bottom halfway through the baking time. Cool the cookies and transfer to a plate. Store in an airtight container at room temperature.